A Partnership of Mind and Body:
BIOFEEDBACK

LARRY KETTELKAMP

A Partnership of Mind and Body:

BIOFEEDBACK

illustrated with photographs
William Morrow and Company
New York 1976

Library of Congress Cataloging in Publication Data

Kettelkamp, Larry.
    A partnership of mind and body, biofeedback.

    SUMMARY: Discusses biofeedback, a method of mentally controlling involuntary body processes such as blood pressure and brainwave frequency.
    1. Biofeedback training—Juvenile literature.   [1. Biofeedback training]
I. Title.
BF319.5.B5K47   152.1'88   76-24818
ISBN 0-688-22088-6
ISBN 0-688-32088-0 lib. bdg.

Photo Credits

J. V. Basmajian, pp. 40, 41; Creative Photography, Ronald Eckert, pp. 15, 31, 39, 51, 53, 59, 62, 64, 76, 77; Donovan Klotzbeacher, p. 19; Jim Moore, p. 58; NIH Gerontology Photo, p. 24; The Menninger Foundation, p. 70.

Contents

The author wishes to thank
the following people
for contributing materials
and offering helpful suggestions:
Lester Fehmi, Ph.D.
J. V. Basmajian, M.D.
Bernard T. Engel, Ph.D.
Alyce M. Green
Elmer E. Green, Ph.D.
Ronald Eckert, Photographer

Biofeedback

Feedback is a constant part of human activity. It is at work for the basketball player practicing jump shots, for the girl using the mirror to put on makeup for a date, for the piano player working out a new song, or the recording artist listening to her latest "take" on tape. These varied activities have one thing in common. The body is learning by observing outside information about itself. The word *feedback* means just that— information returned to the source. The feedback may be auditory: using the ears. It may be tactile: using the sense of touch. Or perhaps it may involve taste, smell, or the sense of balance. This constant feedback of information is something usually taken for granted.

The basketball player watches the path of the ball as he pushes it toward the hoop. If it falls short, he automatically pushes the ball harder the next time. In addition, the player notes how his fingertips, wrists, and arms felt with each shot, and how he jumped and landed. The makeup mirror shows the girl immediately the results of each mark made with eyebrow pencil or eyelash brush. Changes or additions can be quickly calculated. The piano player watches his fingers on the keys to see that they touch the right locations in the right order. If not, he notes the error and sends a new set of instructions to the fingertips. Both the piano player and the recording artist are also getting sound patterns as feedback. The pianist hears the sounds as he makes them, and the recording artist listens to the results of each tape-recorded "take" in order to improve the next one.

Imagine how difficult this would be if for some reason the feedback information were not available. Suppose the basketball player has his eyes closed or is forced to shoot baskets in a dark room. Suppose the girl has no mirror. Or imagine that the pianist and the recording artist can neither see their fingers and instruments nor hear the sounds they produce. With these obstacles the learning task seems all but impossible.

This lack of feedback is just the situation, however, with many activities that are out of reach inside the body itself. Although there is a part of the human nervous system that regulates breathing, heartbeat, digestion, body temperature, blood pressure, and a host of other functions, it seems strangely automatic and out of reach. There have always been scattered reports of holy men or mystics who, through years of concentration, learned to control their heartbeat or body temperature. But most people believed such control was impossible—that is, until the modern discovery of a new approach. In dozens of hospitals, clinics, laboratories, and offices around the world, people of all ages and types are now learning to control what was out of reach before. The secret is partly modern technology. Electronic medical equipment is being used to give an individual a picture, sound, or signal on the *outside* of something happening *inside* his body.

This new method of feeding the body changing information about itself is called "biofeedback." The term combines the word *bio,* meaning body, with the word *feedback,* meaning information returned to itself. The internal information is translated into signals that can be easily understood. Lights or tones tell a person he is producing particular electrical brain waves. A bell rings when his heart goes too fast. A meter needle reflects his deepest emotions, or a series of clicks tells him that tiny muscle cells, which he cannot see, are firing.

The surprising discovery is that in many cases this new information may be enough for a person to learn to change his brain waves, slow his heart, alter his emotional reactions, or fire his hidden muscle cells whenever he wants to. How it works almost seems less important than the fact that it *does* work. The information itself is the teacher.

With the computer age, electronic feedback was developed for certain computer systems. The automatic pilot on a large aircraft is a good example. It is programmed to monitor all of the information needed for flight control—air speed, altitude, flying angle, and the direction of flight. All of these facts are constantly compared with the desired flight plan, and through a series of small corrections the plane is kept to its ideal course. The procedure is automatic because of the changing information fed back constantly to the computer. Biofeedback works in a similar way, except that in this case the technical equipment serves the human mind as it gains complete control of its own body through exact and up-to-the-minute information about what is happening within.

The principle of biofeedback training can be applied to almost any body-mind activity. However, the routines tend to fall into five basic kinds of control: body temperature, heart rate and blood pressure, muscles, skin response, and mind control. Temperature control makes use of a thermister to detect changes in temperature in various parts of the body. By noticing the at-first accidental changes in temperature, subjects learn to warm or cool parts of the body. Heart-rate and blood-pressure control are measured by a stethoscope and an electrocardiograph machine, and a pressure cuff that checks ongoing changes in blood pressure. These may enable subjects to lower blood pressure or alter their heartbeat. Muscle activity and tension in any part of the body, even the activity of single nerve cells, can be measured with implanted wires or surface electrodes, and feedback tones are used to convey this changing information. Skin response, a measurement of the skin's changing electrical resistance, amounts to a kind of outside mirror of the emotions and the body changes that accompany them. Mind control is learned through a new awareness of mental states associated with measured changes in various brain waves.

The discovery of biofeedback came in many places almost at the same time. A simple idea, it had been almost ignored by modern science. In recent years pioneer biofeedback scientists have made a number of intriguing discoveries in each of the five general categories. Mind and body, working as reflections of each other, are indeed becoming amazing partners.

Temperature Guides

Some of the first biofeedback discoveries were made partly by accident. One of them grew out of an experiment at The Menninger Foundation in Topeka, Kansas, testing some aspects of Autogenic Training, a system of therapy developed in Europe in the early 1900's. Subjects following Autogenic Training repeat appropriate phrases and visualizations to gain gradual control over certain body processes. For example, typical phrases for increasing warmth in the hands might be, "My arms and hands are relaxed and warm." "Warmth is flowing into my hands."

Psychologists Elmer Green, Alyce Green, and E. Dale Walters of the Voluntary Controls Project were researching this approach at The Menninger Foundation. Results were encouraging, and it seemed that they could be accelerated by giving the subjects information about what was actually happening inside their bodies as they tried to make these changes. Accordingly, Dr. Green began to design a special Biofeedback Temperature Trainer.

By coincidence one of the volunteers in this research was a woman with frequent migraine headaches. These headaches usually develop on one side of the head, are very painful, and last hours or even days. During one of the training sessions the woman had a migraine-headache attack. After going through the exercise for increasing warmth in the hands, she sat quietly in a darkened and comfortable room for several minutes. Dr. Green was watching the record of her hand temperature as it appeared on the polygraph paper in the control room. He noticed that her hands were suddenly getting warmer, quickly rising ten degrees in temperature. When he asked her what had happened in the last minute or two she said, "How did you know my headache went away?" Surprisingly, when the hand temperature changed, the migraine headache vanished. There had been a sudden flow of warm blood released into her hands, which resulted in their dramatic rise in temperature.

The researchers were intrigued by what had happened and mentioned it to some of their colleagues in the research department. Two people who suffered from migraine headaches asked if they might try the hand-temperature training. Several of the new temperature trainers had been built by this time, and the two volunteers used the training system, which the Menninger team called Autogenic Feedback Training. It was a combina-

tion of the autogenic suggestions with temperature biofeedback. In addition to using the phrases, each subject
would have a thermister, a temperature-measuring device,
attached to the middle finger of one hand. A needle
swinging along a dial on the temperature meter would instantly show them any change in hand temperature and
the direction of the change. When the mental suggestions
worked and the hands became warmer, the difference
would show on the meter.

The two volunteers tried the new system. One was
partly helped, and the other was able to eliminate the
migraine attacks completely. Interested in these results,
Dr. Joseph Sargent, head of Internal Medicine at The
Menninger Foundation, set up a pilot study with headache victims. Seventy-five volunteers, self-referred or re-
ferred by their physicians, were accepted as subjects.
All suffered from migraine or other headache problems.
After a complete physical examination and laboratory
study, each volunteer received instruction in using a temperature trainer that showed the difference in temperature between the forehead and the right index finger.
The subjects combined use of the trainer with the autogenic suggestions for relaxation and warmth. Each subject had a training session once or twice a week until he
or she had learned to produce the desired response on the
meter and at the same time to sense the warmth in the

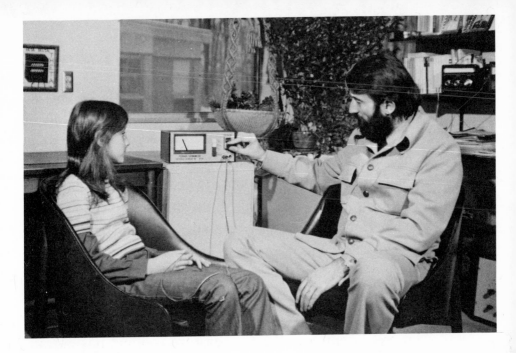

Above:
Dr. Lester Fehmi adjusts temperature-biofeedback monitor.
Below:
Subject reacts with pleasure
as meter needle shows her hand is getting warmer.

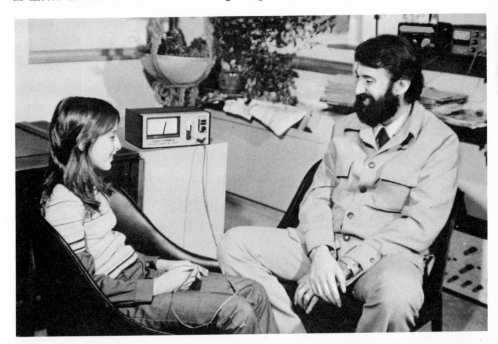

hands. Then the volunteers began to practice part of the time without the training device and usually no longer needed it after a month's time. All were encouraged to continue daily practice and to use their hand-warming technique to control tension and headache. The minimum follow-up period with the volunteers was a year.

Migraine headaches are associated with cold hands. When the subjects learn to warm the hands they are learning to "turn off" tension, to decrease the blood in the vessels of the head and to direct blood flow to the hands. In some way the brain has readjusted the circulatory system, and the temperature training has encouraged this needed change.

Dr. David Danskin, at the University of Kansas in Manhattan, Kansas, reported the case of a mathematics professor who was a migraine sufferer. The woman had been a victim of migraine headaches since she was a child, and as an adult she had often been forced to leave work and go home with severe migraines. The woman always had a warning of an oncoming headache. It was the sense of a smell like ammonia. This is called an "aura" and is typical of many migraine sufferers. Before biofeedback training she would know a headache was coming but be unable to do anything about it. After her hand-warming training, whenever the aura occurred, she would go home and lie down to use her hand-warming exercises. Often the headache would disappear before becoming severe. Later on she was able simply to sit quietly in her office for about fifteen minutes, and by concentrating on warming her hands she could avoid the headache. Now her training has become a habit. Whenever she has the warning aura, she gives herself the mental suggestion, "Go back down, blood." Her body responds and the headache is avoided.

The temperature technique developed by the Menninger team was tested further by Ian Wickramasekera, but without the use of autogenic phrases. Two schoolteachers had tried a number of ways of relieving painful migraines including visits to a medical clinic and drugs that had been prescribed. They agreed to try biofeedback. A thermister was attached to the forehead of each patient to measure temperature, and a second temperature thermister was fastened to the middle finger of the right hand. Both teachers learned to warm their hands within a few sessions, while their foreheads cooled at the same time. As training continued the headaches for both patients occurred less often and were less intense. Three months after the training the teachers still were able to control most headaches with the temperature system and had stopped taking aspirin almost entirely.

One of the most fascinating temperature experiments was done with a visitor to The Menninger Foundation.

During his work with biofeedback and autogenic training, Dr. Green received an interesting offer. A friend, Dr. Daniel Ferguson, told Green of an Indian yogi, Swami Rama. Reportedly the swami could control a number of involuntary functions. Dr. Ferguson brought Swami Rama to the lab.

To the amazement of the researchers, the swami changed the temperature of one hand so that one side of the hand was ten degrees warmer than the other side of the same hand! Within a few minutes the left part of his palm was rosy red and warm, while the right part was cold and gray. The swami had developed this unusually fine control through years of yogic meditation and concentration. The test with Swami Rama suggested that body-temperature control could be developed to a very exact degree. And the success of biofeedback temperature training with average individuals indicated that apparently such learning is possible with weeks rather than years of training.

In later temperature-feedback experiments, it has been found that very specific control indeed can be learned. A. H. Roberts trained a group of subjects during sixteen daily sessions. With temperature-feedback information, the subjects learned to produce a difference in temperature between the index fingers of each hand. They could make the right index finger warmer than the left, then switch to make the left warmer than the right, and finally reverse the difference once again. In another experiment researchers Lynch, Hama, and Kohn, working in the laboratory of psychologist Neal Miller, had similar results with two ten-year-old youngsters. In this case the subjects learned to control and alternate the temperature difference between the first and third fingers of the same hand by using temperature feedback. The young trainees had shown a control of hand temperature similar to that demonstrated by Swami Rama at The Menninger Foundation.

A simple hand-warming experiment
with a household thermometer.
Hold thumb against the glass bulb.
Allow about ten minutes
for an accurate reading.
Average hand temperature
will range
from a cool 75° F.
to a warm 95° F.

Controlling Heart Rate and Blood Pressure

One of the most fascinating areas for biofeedback study is that of the human heart rate and blood pressure. Some of this research was done at The Menninger Foundation with Swami Rama. In addition to body-temperature control, the swami was also able to demonstrate unusual control of his heartbeat. For these measurements the swami was connected to an electrocardiograph machine, called "EKG" for short. The machine would monitor the heart and provide ongoing pen tracings beat by beat. While hooked to the machine Swami Rama was able to increase his heartbeat and slow it down. He sat motionless in his yogic posture as he did so.

After several days of testing, the swami announced that he would try to stop his heart for three or four minutes in the laboratory for the researchers the next morning. Dr. Green and his wife, Alyce, working as a team, wanted to avoid unnecessary dangers in the experiments. They told the swami that if he could stop his heart for ten seconds that would be quite enough for a successful demonstration.

In the morning the swami was wired to the EKG. Alyce Green was in the control room, and the swami asked her to watch the tracings and call out "that's all" when it was time for the demonstration to be over. Again sitting motionless in his yogic posture, the swami made a few trial runs at speeding and slowing his heart. He then said, "I am going to give a shock; do not be alarmed." He meant that what he was going to do would shock the researchers, and he didn't want to alarm them.

Soon came the call from the control room, "That's all!" Dr. Green hurried in to look at the electrocardiogram. According to the tracings, instead of stopping, the heart had jumped suddenly from around 70 beats per minute to around 300 beats per minute. Although the heartbeat had changed to a rapid flutter instead of stopping, in this state no blood fills the heart chambers. The swami had stopped his heart from pumping blood for seventeen seconds.

Whatever may be the exact definition of a "stopped heart," the swami had demonstrated an unusual type of control and had created a state in which a person ordinarily would have passed out. Although the heart stopping was dramatic, perhaps more important was the swami's voluntary control of the rate of his heartbeat without other changes in body activity.

Could ordinary people without the yogic training learn to control their heartbeats? The idea had actually been tested earlier in an intriguing set of experiments by another researcher, Bernard Engel, a psychologist with the National Institute on Aging.

The sessions took place in a quiet room of his laboratory in Baltimore, Maryland. A patient would lie quietly on a hospital bed. On a display panel a yellow light glowed. Suddenly a red light flashed on and the yellow light went out. Within a second, or less than the space of a single heartbeat, a green light went on. Soon it, too, went off, and the patient smiled as the yellow light again glowed steadily. The patient was a victim of heart disease and was one of eight in the unique study begun by Dr. Engel.

All eight patients had a kind of uneven heartbeat called PVC, an abbreviation that stands for "premature ventricular contraction." One of the heart's chambers contracts or pumps too soon, throwing the beat off rhythm. Some patients do not feel anything unusual; others feel as if the heart skips a beat sometimes.

Engel and a physician, Dr. Theodore Weiss, designed a clever system to help the PVC patients train their heartbeats back to normal. Electrodes were taped to the chest over the heart. The heart pulses were fed to electronic equipment that timed the heart rate. If it was too slow, a green light went on. This meant "go—get your heart moving a little faster." If the heart was running ahead of the desired rate, a red light would flash on. This meant "slow your heart down a little." If the heart was beating at about the right rate, the yellow light would go on, meaning "everything is OK." And if a PVC occurred, there was a special warning. The red light flashed, followed quickly by a flash of the green light.

As the patients followed the light signals they gradually learned to control their heart rhythms and eliminate the PVC's to some extent. To make the improvements permanent, the light signals were turned off for short periods and later for longer periods. Five out of the eight patients made definite improvement. One woman eliminated the bothersome PVC's almost entirely. She was able to stop using the drugs with which doctors had tried to control the condition. Even three years after the training her heart was still beating normally.

The patients were asked what they were thinking about when their heart control was working. For some, the best results came by trying to slow down the heart, while others got a smoother heartbeat by trying to speed it up a bit. One patient imagined a rubber ball bouncing to make the heart go faster. One imagined shifting his heart

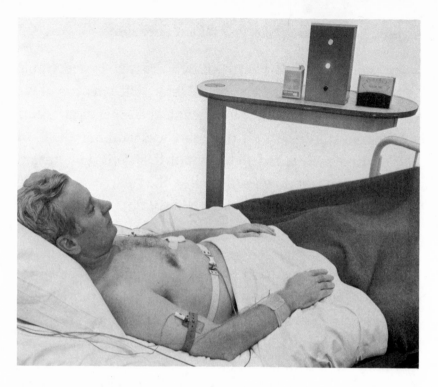

A technician demonstrates experiments in which
patients are taught to control abnormal heart rhythms
at Baltimore's Gerontology Research Center.
Panel of colored lights shows subject his progress.

to the left to gain control. Another imagined moving
back and forth in a swing to slow it down. Although all
of the patients used the same "traffic light" feedback
system, each one worked out his own method of achiev-
ing the regular heart rhythm.

Of almost equal importance in the health of the circulatory system is the proper control of blood pressure and blood flow in various parts of the body. As fine inner adjustments are constantly being made, the amount and balance of this pressure and flow are changed. For example, recall the embarrassment you felt at a pointed remark that caused the blood to rush to your face. You could feel the sudden warmth, and you knew that everyone could see the rosy flush in your cheeks and forehead. You wished it hadn't happened; the blush was a dead giveaway. It let everyone know how awkward you felt.

The blush is triggered by a part called the "hypothalamus" deep within the brain and is part of the reflex action of the autonomic nervous system, which controls heart rate, breathing, digestion, and changes of blood flow in the body. It is when the tiny blood capillaries at the surface of the body relax and expand, or dilate, that the blood rushes in, causing a blush. For most of us the blush is an occasional awkward reaction. For some people there is a constant overreaction so that blushing is out of control and is a real problem.

Neal Miller, a psychologist working at Rockefeller University in New York, decided to see if blushing could be controlled. For his experiment, Miller chose white rats. Each rat was injected with curare to paralyze the skeletal muscles. A respirator was put over each rat's nose to keep it breathing, and a narrow needle was inserted into a pleasure center of the rat's brain. Although paralyzed, the rat remained conscious, and a small electrical charge would produce a pleasant sensation.

First the rat had to learn how to control blood volume in both ears. If given an electrical pleasure reward for dilating the blood vessels to increase blood flow to the ears, the rat soon learned to repeat this achievement to get the reward. Or if the task was reversed, the rat gradually learned to constrict the blood vessels in the ears to get the pleasure reward. Next the rat was rewarded for creating a difference in blood volume between the two ears. Again the biofeedback stimulus created the desired result. Soon Miller had taught several rats to increase the blood volume in one ear only on cue. That ear would turn a vivid pink while the other ear stayed pale. Miller's white rats had actually learned to blush in one ear.

Blushing in one ear may not seem of much practical value, but another type of circulatory control, that of general blood pressure, is extremely important for human beings. High blood pressure, or hypertension, is one of today's greatest health problems. So Miller turned to human tests. If rats could learn certain internal controls, people ought to do at least as well, although the process might be more complicated. Barry Dworkin, a graduate student working with Miller, set about designing a special blood-pressure apparatus that would provide a constant feedback reading. If people could somehow use biofeed-back to lower their own blood pressure at will, the damage of hypertension might possibly be avoided without the use of drugs.

The usual blood-pressure device in a doctor's office works with a cuff around the arm, which is inflated to block partly the flow of blood through an artery. The pressure in the cuff is compared with the pressure in the artery, and the set of fixed readings that results reflects the blood pressure at that particular instant.

What was needed for biofeedback was a way to watch the blood pressure continuously from heartbeat to heartbeat. Dworkin started with the usual pressure cuff. An automatic pump was added to keep the cuff inflated to just the right pressure. In place of the usual stethoscope, a tiny microphone was placed against the arm inside the cuff. Electrodes were placed on various parts of the body to monitor heart rate and breathing. The electrical signals appeared on an oscilloscope, and a polygraph pen traced the pulses on a roll of graph paper.

The tests included volunteers who were perfectly healthy as well as those with high blood pressure. Each volunteer lay quietly on his back in a darkened room. Whenever the pressure reading went down, a tone would come on in the room. As the subjects learned to lower their blood pressure, the equipment was adjusted so that a greater drop in pressure was needed to make the tone come on. Results were fair, but the successful subjects still had some trouble when they were away from the laboratory.

A group of volunteers were patients from Bellevue Hospital, associated with the New York University Medical Center. One of the best subjects turned out to be a young woman who earlier had been rushed to the emergency room of another hospital. Robin Bielski had headache pains that would not go away, she could not sleep, had a stiff neck, and was constantly dizzy. In the hospital it was discovered that Miss Bielski had severe bleeding inside her head. An operation was quickly performed to remove the pressure. After the operation Robin Bielski was in a coma. When she finally became conscious, she could not control the left side of her body, and her blood pressure was abnormally high.

Miss Bielski came to the New York University facility for rehabilitation after her stroke. Through physical therapy she gradually improved the control of her body muscles, but she had to stay in a wheelchair. And in spite of the use of special drugs, her blood pressure was dangerously high. The doctors decided that most of her trouble had come from the high blood pressure, or hypertension.

Robin Bielski learned of Dr. Miller's experiments with

blood pressure and biofeedback training in the hospital. Barry Dworkin thought she would make a good subject and that they might help her condition, so she began regular work with Dworkin. Miss Bielski's only cue was a beep whenever she was able to follow the directions. Sometimes Dworkin asked her to lower her blood pressure. If she did, she heard a beep. Sometimes she was asked to raise it to get the beep. Dworkin even asked her to make it go up and down continuously.

After a little over a month Miss Bielski was able to lower her blood pressure consistently. Miller and Dworkin asked her doctor if she could be taken off the special drugs. At first her blood pressure started to shoot up again. But within a few days she had learned to lower it without the drugs. Finally she was able to move to her own apartment and simply visit the hospital each day. Soon she was able to live fairly normally, even though she still used the wheelchair. The biofeedback training had given Robin Bielski workable control over her blood pressure.

Sometime later she needed further surgery. Because of this and other problems, she lost most of what she had gained and was placed on medication again. However, after overcoming these problems, Miss Bielski later returned for retraining with biofeedback. She was able to relearn to a considerable extent how to control her blood pressure and could get along well with a minimal dosage of drugs. While Robin Bielski was eventually successful in controlling her blood pressure, about twenty-six other patients receiving similar biofeedback training did much less well. The researchers concluded that perhaps either the training techniques or the method of selecting patients would have to be improved.

In a more recent blood-pressure training experiment, five patients who had all suffered from high blood pressure for at least ten years were selected from the Hypertension Clinic of the Baltimore City Hospitals. Psychologist Bernard Engel and Donald Kristt, a physician, devised a three-part program to train the five volunteers.

In the first part the patients took their blood-pressure readings at home and mailed the records to the researchers. In the second part the patients were admitted to the Gerontology Research Center of the Baltimore City Hospitals for three weeks. In the third part the patients returned home and again kept records of their blood pressure.

While in the hospital each patient lay in a bed in a soundproof room. A microphone inside a standard blood-pressure cuff was used to take readings. The patients watched a panel of red, yellow, and green cue lights. If the red light was on, the patient was to try to lower his blood pressure. If the green light was on, he was to try to raise it. The yellow light stayed on as long as the patient was performing properly in each trial.

During the first week the patients were trained to raise their blood pressure. During the second week they were trained to lower it. And in the final week they were trained to raise and lower it alternately within a single

The author tries a hand-warming relaxation routine
with Dr. Lester Fehmi.
Arm pressure cuff and stethoscope can be used
to check blood pressure during the session.

session. The patients were also taught a procedure for lowering blood pressure that they could use later at home. The records from the last week showed that through the biofeedback training all of the patients were able to control their blood pressure, some more effectively than others.

After returning home, the patients were able to keep their blood pressure lower than it had been before. Tests made at the hospital one month and three months after the training suggested that the five patients had retained their abilities to both raise and lower their blood pressure.

Other blood-pressure training programs have demonstrated that biofeedback can sometimes be an effective tool. Additional studies have been done at Lafayette Clinic in Detroit and at Nova University in Fort Lauderdale, Florida. Not all tests are successful, but doctors have been encouraged by the positive results with blood-pressure control through biofeedback training.

Muscle Monitors

Another challenge for biofeedback is the control of muscles of the body. The outer skeletal muscles can, of course, be trained through visual feedback. We can see the results of an arm, leg, or body movement and make corrections as we learn to ride bicycles, drive cars, and practice hundreds of other skills. Some of the inner muscles, such as those in the larynx, are subject to indirect control. The wish or thought of speaking or singing is what activates the breathing muscles and vocal cords. Here again feedback is at work since we can hear the results and to some extent correct the sound patterns to improve performance.

However, the smooth muscles of the body, those of throat, stomach, and other organs, seem beyond the reach of voluntary control. There is little or no outside feedback from such muscle groups, which act mainly by reflex. Usually the conscious mind is not aware of these inner functions at all. How can biofeedback be used to gain control over these out-of-reach muscles?

Most recent theories about how the body and mind work have come from a group of psychologists called "behaviorists." An accepted principle of theirs is that learning results from the body reacting to a changing stimulus in the environment. The physiologist Pavlov proved that a dog could be conditioned to produce saliva in his mouth when a bell was rung. First the bell was sounded, and then the dog would immediately be given a piece of meat. This procedure was repeated until the dog associated the bell with the food reward. Soon, even when the food did not follow, the dog would salivate simply at the sound of the bell.

Sometime later psychologist Neal Miller, then working at Yale University, decided to go a step further. He divided some thirsty dogs into two groups. In the first group each dog received water whenever the saliva in the mouth happened to increase. In the other group the dogs got the water only when saliva happened to decrease. The first group of dogs learned to increase saliva regularly to get the water reward; the second group of dogs learned regularly to decrease saliva to get the water.

Working with another researcher, Leo DiCara, Miller next chose to try to teach laboratory rats to control some of their inner functions. So that the outer body muscles could have no effect on the results, Miller and DiCara paralyzed the rats with curare. The rats were kept breathing artificially, and through a tiny needle each rat received a small electrical pleasure reward deep in the brain when it performed properly. Through these simple pleasure rewards Miller taught his paralyzed but conscious rats to increase and decrease their heartbeat, blood pressure, and even digestion. His work was an ingenious demonstration of biofeedback at work.

These new experiments suggested that inner control of muscles and glands could be learned under certain conditions. But some of the animal experiments were complicated. And how could anyone tell what the animals experienced during such training?

Looking around for a simple biofeedback experiment to try on himself, Neal Miller came up with a novel idea. How about ear wiggling? Certainly ear wiggling is a curiosity for human beings. Although animals move their ears about in various ways responding to sounds and signals, most people lack this ability, probably because it is not a matter of survival. But Miller was one of the few people who could wiggle his ears. However, both ears would always move at the same time. Miller wondered if he could learn to wiggle only one ear. And since ear wiggling seemed beyond the usual reach of muscle training, he became fascinated with the challenge. Miller's unusual experiment was described in the book *Visceral Learning* by Gerald Jonas.

In 1901, a researcher named J. H. Bair actually had designed a biofeedback experiment along similar lines. He used a crude machine to trace the tiny movements of one ear as squiggly lines on a moving cylinder. By watching these mechanically magnified tracings of almost unnoticed ear movements, he gradually taught himself to increase the movements and to learn to wiggle one ear. And he taught others to learn the same trick by watching their own ear squiggles. But Bair's curious experiment had been forgotten by most people, and Dr. Miller came up with the same simple idea independently. Instead of setting up a complicated electronic measuring device, Miller chose to use only his bathroom mirror. He reasoned that if he watched his ears while trying to wiggle only one, he could immediately see if he was successful. The mirror would provide the feedback information.

Miller tried various approaches. Since he could wiggle both ears together, he tried to be aware of the muscle feelings as he did so. Then he tried to wiggle only one ear by pretending that these feelings were present on only the right side of his head. Then he imagined that the left side of his head was cold and numb so that the left ear would not respond. No luck. But Miller would not give up, and day after day he spent a few minutes in front of the mirror watching and trying. Finally he concentrated on producing only a tiny movement of the right ear. When he detected a slight movement, even by accident, he tried to increase it a little each day. But whenever the left ear also moved, he had to stop and go back to the beginning again. Very gradually with the use of the mirror, the right ear began to respond alone. Soon it was making large twitches. Now, without looking in the mirror at all, Miller could make his right ear wiggle whenever he wanted it to, while the left ear stayed perfectly still. Through the simplest of experiments, Dr. Miller had trained a set of partly involuntary muscles.

On a more sophisticated level another muscle feedback experiment took place in the laboratory of Dr. J. V. Basmajian. Sixteen volunteers had been chosen for biofeedback experiments in the control of single muscle units. On each volunteer two threadlike wires were inserted at the back of the thumb near the wrist. Dr. Basmajian used a special hypodermic needle to insert the wires. The insertion was like a vaccination shot except that in this case wires were inside the needle. Tiny hooks on the ends of the wires helped them to stay in place inside the thumb muscle when the needle was withdrawn. They could easily be removed at the end of the experiment. The procedure was no more uncomfortable than getting a shot at the doctor's office.

The muscle cells near the wires inside the thumb were triggered by a single motor nerve cell in the spinal cord.

The electrical activity was measured by a machine called an "electromyograph." The firing of this spinal nerve cell stimulated only its particular small group of muscle cells in the thumb, causing them to contract. But the activity was so slight that no movement of the thumb could be seen. From each volunteer the muscle electrical activity was sent to an amplifier. Pulses appeared on an oscilloscope and were translated into taps, or clicks, which came over a loudspeaker. Also the pulses were captured on a tape recorder so that they could be studied again later. Each pulse, or click, meant that the spinal nerve cell had fired a charge to the muscle cells.

One of the volunteers became especially proficient. The experimenters would seat him comfortably in a chair and put the thumb wires in place. Sounds like drumbeats could be heard from the loudspeaker. First there was a slow and regular tapping, next a sound like the galloping of horses' hooves. Then there were fast taps like the rapid roll on a snare drum. "Let's hear the galloping hooves again," the experimenter could ask the volunteer. Almost immediately the imitation galloping taps would come from the loudspeaker.

Although this was an unusual performance by a prize subject, actually all the volunteers were fairly successful. Within half an hour of being rigged up with the thumb wires, all learned to relax the thumb muscle when they wanted to. In addition, they all learned to "turn on" the single tiny nerve-and-muscle motor unit to which the wires were sensitive. After learning this control, all of the subjects were asked to control another separate motor unit. Most succeeded. Some of the volunteers went on to learn isolated control of three, four, or even five motor units. Like the prize subject, they could choose which motor unit they wanted to fire and prevent the others from firing. And they could fire the different units at the request of the experimenter.

Electromyograph (EMG) needle swings to left
and tone decreases in pitch
as a volunteer reduces muscle tension in his forearm.

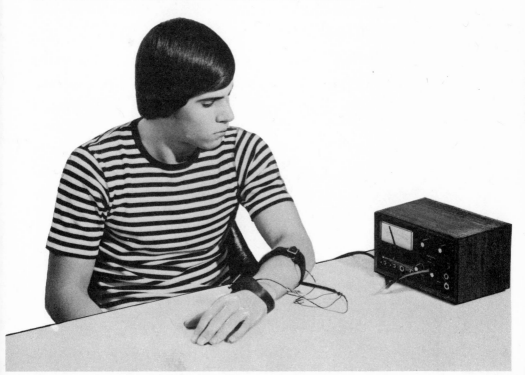

These talented subjects learned a collection of tricks with their new muscle control. They were able to produce slow firing and fast firing and complicated rhythms. Some of the patterns occurred accidentally at first, but the gifted volunteers found out how to repeat them. All of the volunteers gained a surprising amount of control.

Dr. John Basmajian records observations
and checks equipment used to monitor signals
from subject working with arm-muscle biofeedback.

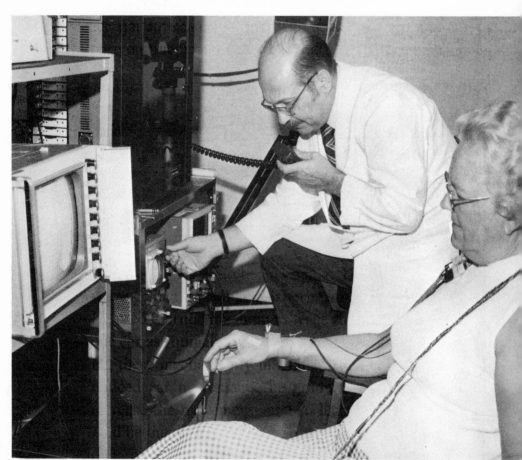

They seemed to get the best results from hearing the sounds of their own muscle units firing. When tested after the biofeedback signals had been turned off, three of the volunteers could still turn on the motor units they wanted to just by thinking about it. They weren't aware of how they did it, but the willful control had become a habit.

New portable muscle trainer developed by Dr. Basmajian gives automatic light signal to patient when he activates muscle to lift his foot.

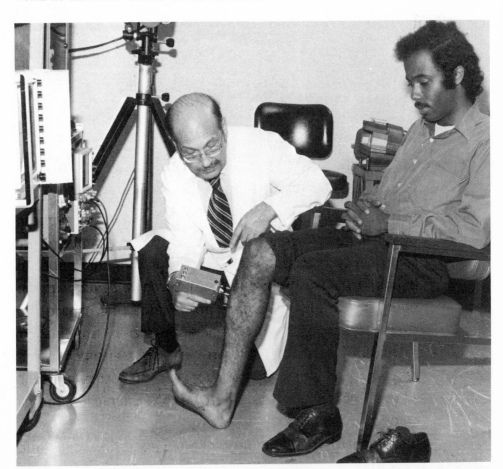

The Voluntary Controls Project of the Research De-partment at The Menninger Foundation used muscle feedback for deep relaxation. The experiments were de-signed by Elmer and Alyce Green, E. Dale Walters, and Dr. Gardner Murphy, at that time head of the Menninger Research Department. The Menninger team used a screen electrode placed on the forearm. The surface electrode would pick up signals from a wide group of forearm muscles.

Each subject sat in a comfortable chair. The electrode was connected to an amplifier, and the amount of muscle tension was fed back to the subject on a meter with a needle pointer. The subjects were instructed to bring the meter needle down to zero. During about twenty minutes of relaxation with the meter, seven out of twenty-one sub-jects learned to lower the rate of muscle firing to about six or seven per second. When they were able to lower the rate still further, it would suddenly drop to zero. Like Basmajian's subjects, some of the Menninger volunteers could learn to turn off muscle tension entirely. And eleven of the twenty-one subjects achieved low tension levels but not single motor-unit firing. One theory about muscles was that body muscles always had some tension even when not doing special jobs. Now biofeedback was showing the old idea to be false. Muscles not being used for work could indeed be totally free of tension.

The Menninger researchers noticed that the subjects who were moving toward the zero level reported strange body changes. Subjects said that their arms felt like a bag of cement or a ton of lead. One person remarked that his arm felt "as if it is moving away from me." Another comment was, "I had to look at it to see if it was still in the same place." With a little instruction and practice, subjects could think of the right forearm as being detached from the rest of their muscular system. The left arm, leg, or neck muscles could be tensed without significant increase of tension in the right arm.

Two psychologists at the University of Colorado Medical Center teamed up to do some related research on muscle tension. Johann Stoyva was a sleep researcher interested in relaxation techniques. Thomas Budzinski was an electronics engineer as well as a psychologist. The two researchers chose the common tension headache for their studies. Such a headache usually includes tension across the forehead as well as tension and pain in neck muscles. The tension headache seems caused by stress from worries and fears.

For their feedback measurements, Stoyva and Budzinski chose the frontalis muscle of the forehead, which is involved in tension headaches and is a muscle over which most people have little or no control. The researchers ran a newspaper ad asking for volunteers who suffered from tension headache. There were more replies than they could handle. A group was chosen for a series of tests. With electrodes in place on the forehead, the muscle tension was monitored electrically. Compared with the average person, the headache victims registered more tension in the frontalis muscle.

A relaxation program was begun. One group of volunteers listened to their own muscle-feedback signal. The tension was heard as a series of clicks. Slower clicks meant lower tension. At first a small drop in tension would cause a marked slowing of the clicks. As the group learned to relax the muscle, the equipment was set so that a greater drop in tension was needed to get the same result. Through a series of sessions the group learned to reduce the muscle tension dramatically. As the frontalis became more relaxed, the relaxation began to spread to the neck muscles and other parts of the body.

To make sure that the biofeedback was responsible, other subjects were given feedback sounds that had nothing to do with the actual muscle tension, either random sounds or constant low tones. Probably because they were quiet and comfortable, these control subjects all showed some relaxation of the frontalis muscle. But the muscle tension was lowered much further and more quickly by those who were hearing the actual changes as they occurred. By the fourth week, the volunteers getting accurate feedback had reduced their headaches by about 75 percent.

Medical doctors have found muscle biofeedback good therapy following paralysis or a stroke. Dr. Joseph Brudny is director of a new Sensory Feedback Therapy Unit at the Rehabilitation and Research Center of the Institute for the Crippled and Disabled in New York. A pilot study with thirty-six patients with some form of paralysis showed that thirty-four were greatly improved through feedback training.

A young electrician had been paralyzed from the neck down. Using muscle feedback over a period of several weeks, he became able to move his hands and arms for shaving, eating, and other tasks. A woman patient had not been able to move her head. For seven years it had been locked to one side, and other forms of treatment had not helped. After four training sessions with muscle feedback, she had learned to relax the large neck muscle that turns the head, simply by listening to the clicks from electrodes fastened to her neck. By lowering the rate of the clicks, proper muscle balance returned, and she could move her head normally.

A portable muscle-feedback device has been developed by John Basmajian and a team of doctors and therapists at Emory University Regional Rehabilitation Research and Training Center in Atlanta, Georgia. It has been especially tested with patients who, because of accident or paralysis, have difficulty pulling the foot up into its normal angle for walking on the heel and toe. Twenty patients were divided into two groups of ten. Each group received special exercise training with a therapist three times a week for five weeks. In addition, one of the groups used the portable muscle monitor regularly as part of the training routine. On the average both groups made some improvement. But the group working with biofeedback made about twice as much improvement in foot control and walking as the control group.

Muscle feedback has also proved effective with speech problems. When youngsters learn to read, the words are first spoken out loud. Later they do not use the voice and read silently. But for some people, the vocal muscles continue to respond, creating an annoying habit called "subvocalization." Muscle feedback has proved very effective in correcting this problem. Vibrations from the throat are amplified so that the reader can hear them clearly. In one such test with a group of vocalizers, most of the subjects reduced subvocalization completely within five minutes. Follow-up tests at one month and three months later showed no return of the problem. In another experiment forty-three college students were able to stop throat sounds within a one-hour training session. Another group of readers who did not receive the feedback sounds showed no change. But when this second group also received a one-hour muscle feedback session, they all learned to stop vocalizing when reading to themselves.

The Voice of the Skin

As early as 1888 a French scientist named Féré discovered that the body's resistance to electricity changed constantly at the surface of the skin. He thought that the changes reflected emotional reactions. At the turn of the century psychologist Carl Jung also experimented with measurements of the skin's electrical resistance. The measured changes did indeed seem to follow changing emotions.

Jung began a series of novel experiments with his patients. Each subject was wired to a recorder in order to monitor changes in electrical skin resistance. Jung gave the patient a word-association test by reading an unrelated group of words. Those words that caused the patient to react emotionally triggered a change in the electrical skin resistance. Jung felt he had come upon a practical way of measuring the innermost feelings of his patients, feelings they might not even be aware of on the conscious level.

At first most psychologists thought that such signals

were nothing more than primitive responses from the autonomic nervous system, and little attention was given to Jung's idea. However, a few experimenters continued, and eventually others became interested in these strange skin signals. One of the first practical applications was in the field of lie detection. Though the science is not an exact one, a trained operator can analyze the skin responses to try to determine the guilt or innocence of a witness or criminal suspect. Just how revealing these skin reactions can be was demonstrated to me by a personal experience with such a machine.

In this case the lie-detection operator was psychologist Lester Fehmi. I arranged to visit his office in a building of the Medical Center in Princeton, New Jersey. Dr. Fehmi had a wide array of electronic equipment used for biofeedback training along with psychotherapy. In order to test my skin reactions, Dr. Fehmi pressed a tiny pad against my first finger and held it in place with a strip of tape around the finger. Another pad was fastened to my middle finger. From the finger pads, wires ran to a box about the size of a hi-fi amplifier, with a meter needle facing me. The machine was measuring galvanic skin response, or GSR for short.

Next Dr. Fehmi set some knobs on the machine so that the meter needle began to bounce a little and a low-pitched whine came out of the loudspeaker. He started to ask me questions about myself. As I replied the whining sound changed, sometimes going up and sometimes dropping lower like a small siren. As the tone went up, so did the needle on the meter. Some of my answers were followed by a strong swing of the needle and change of tone, others by little or no change at all.

"I'll bet I can guess a number you have chosen in your mind," said Dr. Fehmi. I agreed to try the game. He explained that I was to choose a number from one to five and to imagine I was seeing this number, but to say nothing about it. "Can you picture the number in your head now?" he asked. I answered that I could. He then asked me to say "no" to every question he asked for the next few minutes. "Is your number zero?" "No." "Is it six?" I thought these questions were odd, since we both knew the number was between one and five. Then he began to ask the numbers between one and five. "Is it two? Is it four? Is it one?" After each question he paused to see what the reaction was on the meter. He kept mixing the numbers up and repeated them many times. Finally he stopped and said, "I would guess that your mental number was two. Is that correct?" I had to admit that it was.

Although the reactions varied, some of the time there had been a slightly higher tone and greater needle swing when he asked me about the number two. When I answered "no," I knew my statement was false. Since we both knew that the number was neither zero nor six, he had used those numbers to test my reaction to neutral numbers. By asking me several times about the number two along with all the other numbers, he could average out the reactions. His conclusion had been correct. But the reactions were not great, and there was certainly a chance that his guess might be wrong.

I could easily imagine how uncomfortable I might be if I were a suspect being questioned about a crime. How-

A subject watches his delayed autonomic reactions
on meter of the GSR monitor
as he responds to questions by Dr. Fehmi.

ever, when the GSR is used for personal therapy, the subject who is connected to the machine can see the meter as well as hear the changing tone. Thus, he is instantly aware of his own conscious and subconscious reactions to particular questions and topics.

In general, the GSR registers neither "true" nor "false" responses but simply the degree of emotional reaction to a particular topic. Emotional reactions cause subtle changes within the body. Feelings of arousal or stress trigger sweat-gland activity at the surface, and the change in skin resistance mirrors this activity. A low response indicates that the subject feels comfortable with that idea.

A key use of the GSR is for desensitization. Suppose someone has been bitten by a snake and since that time has had a terrible fear of snakes out of proportion to any real danger. The answer can be desensitization. The patient is shown relatively harmless pictures of whatever it is that triggers his fear reactions. By seeing the pictures repeatedly and discussing them calmly in a safe place, the patient gradually reacts in a more normal way. With biofeedback, desensitization has become faster and more efficient.

For example, the person who is afraid of snakes is hooked up to the GSR. In a comfortable chair in a quiet room he can hear the tone that reflects his reactions. A lowering of the tone signal lets him know that he is emo-

Above:
A subject uses GSR tone to monitor
emotional response during desensitization.
Below:
A subject practices relaxation with GSR machine.

tionally relaxed. Pictures are then projected on a screen. Perhaps the first picture is simply of a coiled rope in the shape of a snake. Then come pictures of harmless garter snakes. Gradually pictures of rattlesnakes or cobras are introduced. Whenever the GSR tone rises to register strong emotional reaction, the pictures are turned off and once again the subject is allowed to relax quietly. Through GSR training the subject will eventually be able to watch even close-up pictures of snakes with open mouths and fangs without registering extreme emotional reactions. Instead, the calm feeling will remain more of the time. The patient has now replaced his extreme fear with a more normal response. Later, when confronted with real snakes, he is emotionally prepared to handle the situation.

The combination of biofeedback and pictures can also help people who are afraid of other people. An employee may be afraid of a boss who loses his temper. Or a wife may overreact to an angry husband. If there is no real danger but the fear becomes a habit, normal functioning may be almost impossible for the person. In these cases slide pictures of angry faces are used with the GSR monitor. The pictures pose no real threat, and the sound signal helps the patient learn to lower the emotional response. And again, more normal reactions can be carried over into real-life situations.

Brain Waves
and Mind Control

In the 1920's Hans Berger made the remarkable discovery that the human brain produces special patterns of electrical activity, which tend to correlate with different states of mind or body. He developed a new machine called the "electroencephalograph," or EEG for short. Metal electrodes placed against the head picked up the brain's electrical voltage changes, which were amplified and recorded as pen-and-ink tracings on a moving roll of paper. Tracings were taken of sick people and well people, old and young, people awake and people asleep. The brain seemed constantly active with fluctuations in electrical voltage at a variety of frequencies. A dominant frequency pattern that occurred about ten times per second was the first to interest Berger, and so he gave it the name of the first letter in the Greek alphabet, alpha. A faster brain-wave pattern was named beta, and slower patterns seen before and during sleep were given the names theta and delta respectively.

In 1938, the Nazis put a stop to Berger's inventive research. But sometime later at the University of Chicago, Nathaniel Kleitman and Eugene Aserinsky began using the EEG machine to study the cycles of sleep. Along with other researchers, they demonstrated that there are brain-wave patterns associated with light sleep, deep sleep, and dreams, which repeat during a full night's sleep. When awake, a subject usually generated strong beta waves. When dropping off to sleep, slower and more regular alpha and theta would appear. During deep sleep very slow delta waves predominated. And during dreams waves more closely resembling those of wakefulness or presleep would be present, along with electrical activity from the eyes, which were moving during the dream. Common cycles were noticed, but each person's brain-wave activity also had an individual character, something like a fingerprint.

In the 1950's the psychologist Joe Kamiya was working at the University of Chicago on a government sleep-research project. Fascinated with the large and regular alpha waves that turned on and off in brain-wave tracings, he wondered if people could learn to identify and control these waves. Was there some special feeling that went along with alpha waves? Using head electrodes and the EEG machine, Kamiya experimented with some of his subjects. He told the volunteers that whenever they were producing the special brain wave, their condition would

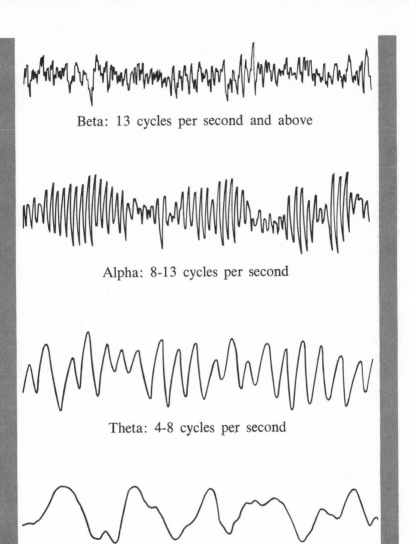

Beta: 13 cycles per second and above

Alpha: 8-13 cycles per second

Theta: 4-8 cycles per second

Delta: 1-4 cycles per second

Typical brain-wave tracings recorded by pen
of the electroencephalograph (EEG) machine.
Frequency groupings are designated
by letters of the Greek alphabet.

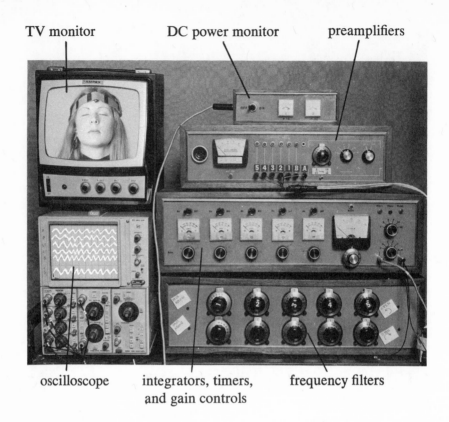

TV monitor   DC power monitor   preamplifiers

oscilloscope   integrators, timers,   frequency filters
and gain controls

An electroencephalograph.

be called state "A." Whenever the brain wave was absent, it would be called state "B." The volunteers would not know which state they were in, but on the signal of a bell ringing once, they were to guess whether they were in state A or B. As soon as a volunteer made a guess, he or she would be told whether or not the guess was correct.

Usually the volunteers guessed right only by chance

during the first hour or so. Then they became right more of the time. Some were right about 60 to 80 percent of the time. A few of the subjects did so well they could guess correctly all of the time.

Since most of the volunteers were able to learn when they were producing alpha and when they were not, Kamiya wondered if they could also control the change from one state to the other. Accordingly, he set up a new system. The subjects were asked to enter the state they had been calling A whenever a bell rang twice. Whenever a bell rang once, they were supposed to enter state B. Most of the subjects could make this change.

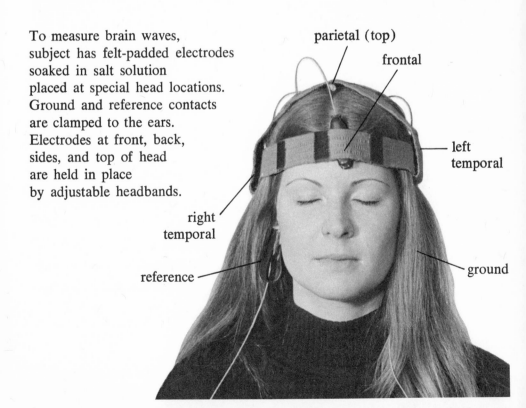

To measure brain waves, subject has felt-padded electrodes soaked in salt solution placed at special head locations. Ground and reference contacts are clamped to the ears. Electrodes at front, back, sides, and top of head are held in place by adjustable headbands.

parietal (top)

frontal

left temporal

right temporal

reference

ground

Then Kamiya experimented with volunteers who had no previous training. They were hooked up to apparatus that sounded a tone when alpha was being produced. Each subject was told, "Hear that tone? That's turned on by your brain wave." Each subject was asked first to keep the tone on and then to keep it off. Again most of the subjects had some success. Kamiya found that simply by knowing the results of their efforts, most of the volunteers could learn to turn their alpha brain waves on or off at will. And with feedback information on the changing strength of their alpha brain waves, the volunteers also could learn to produce stronger alpha.

Without knowing about Joe Kamiya's work, physiologist Barbara Brown was also experimenting in the same direction in the Veterans Administration Hospital lab in Sepulveda, California. Dr. Brown happened to be listening one day to a conversation between two young helpers in the lab. One of the boys was asking if there were some way that the brightly colored images of his imagination could be recorded scientifically. His co-worker did not think so. Whenever he closed his own eyes, all he saw was a gray background.

The discussion triggered a childhood memory for Dr. Brown. She and two friends had sat under a tree talking about how people think. One of her friends said, "I just close my eyes and see everything I want to know. It's all bright and colored and beautiful." Her other friend nodded in agreement. Young Barbara was stunned and ran across the street to her own house in tears. She called to her mother, "They close their eyes and they think in colors. What's wrong with me? I close my eyes and all I see is gray." Years later Barbara Brown recalled the impact of this childhood incident in her book on biofeedback called, *New Mind, New Body*.

But now the three lab workers decided to follow up on the puzzle. They asked hundreds of people about how they imagined things. Sure enough, some people visualized in great detail and color. Others tended not to visualize and usually reported a sort of gray field. Experiments had been going on in the lab recording the brain waves of cats. Why not try recording the brain waves of people who visualized and those who said they didn't?

Tests were set up with volunteers. The brain-wave measurements showed that there was a difference. Visualizers' brain waves reacted strongly to a flashing red light, as if it was an alarm signal. Nonvisualizers reacted very little. Instead, their brain waves moved in rhythm with the flashing of the red light. Perhaps then people's feelings about colors could be measured by recording their brain waves.

Soon Dr. Brown designed a new experiment. Equip-

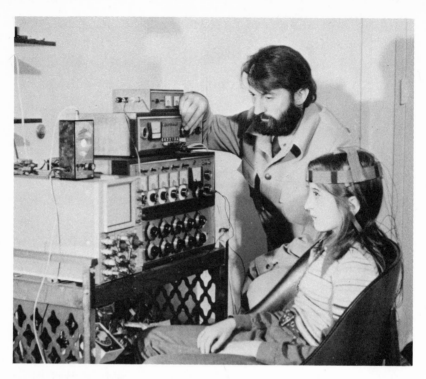

As the subject relaxes, a strobe light blinks
at the frequency of the alpha she is producing.

ment was set up so that whenever a volunteer produced
strong alpha brain waves, a blue light would go on. If
alpha disappeared, the blue light would go off. And
whenever the light was on, it would get brighter when
the alpha waves were strongest. Volunteers were fascinated. At first as they relaxed, the blue light would come
on accidentally as some bursts of alpha were produced.
Soon all were learning to produce more alpha just by

watching the blue light. By following the changing light signals, the subjects were gaining control of a hidden part of themselves that until then was believed to be beyond direct conscious control.

Pleased with the response of volunteers to the lights, Dr. Brown tried another experiment. Visitors to the lab were soon amazed to find among the lights, tones, and wires, an electric-train set. Looking for a way in which biofeedback could be simply demonstrated, Dr. Brown had hit on a novel idea. The train set was battery operated and was safe to connect to the brain-wave monitor. A visitor could be hooked up with electrodes around his head so that he could start and stop the model train with his own brain waves. The tiny brain-wave voltages were amplified to the amount needed to run the train. When alpha brain waves were produced, the train would start up. When alpha stopped, the train would stop. As long as there was regular alpha, the train would continue to run. Reporters and guests all wanted to experiment with the train and were fascinated by the power of their own brain waves.

Because of the success of the "alpha train," Dr. Brown went a step further and rigged up a complete battery-powered racing-car set. In this experiment two people could be hooked up so that they were able to operate the cars with only alpha brain waves. Because of the nature of alpha waves, however, they had to relax in order to produce the alpha that would win the race. The relaxed alpha state took the place of the usual hand-held trigger starter.

The brain waves recorded for these experiments were those that fluctuate from about eight to thirteen cycles per second. Actually the EEG machine with its pen tracings can register brain waves anywhere from only one or two per second up to as many as forty or more cycles per second. There are no definite boundaries between these shifting frequencies, but researchers have

Children demonstrate a setup in which amplified alpha brain waves can power small-scale racing cars.

agreed on the convenient classifications first developed by Hans Berger. Brain waves that fluctuate from one to four cycles per second are called "delta." Those from four to eight cycles are called "theta." Fluctuations from eight to thirteen cycles are called "alpha," and those that are still faster, at about thirteen and above, are grouped together and called "beta."

One of the goals of the researchers was to find whether distinct mental states were associated with particular brain-wave frequencies. An ideal subject for such tests was Swami Rama, who had demonstrated heartbeat and temperature control at The Menninger Foundation earlier. Because of his years of yogic training, the swami seemed able to enter certain mental states at will, and he offered to attempt a series of tests on brain-wave control. For the first two weeks the results were disappointing. The swami had been wired up to the EEG and was asked to produce various mental states. If successful, recordings of predominantly alpha or theta waves should have appeared at various times on the graph paper. Instead, no matter what he was asked to do, the pen tracings showed that the fast beta waves of active attention were predominant.

Eventually the swami himself, without knowing these results, announced that something was wrong, and he had not been able to achieve any of the proper states.

After investigation, the graph paper itself turned out to be the source of the problem. Before the tests, Dr. Elmer Green mentioned to the swami that the polygraph paper cost sixteen dollars a box. The swami admitted that he couldn't get this thought out of his mind, and during the tests all he could think of was the enormous expense as the researchers watched the paper shooting out of the machine. Dr. Green assured the swami that the budget for the project would allow for running the paper continuously for days at a time and that the amount of paper used was nothing to worry about.

Afterward the swami relaxed and in a few fifteen-minute sessions was able to associate his changing mental states with the tone signals of the biofeedback equipment. First he produced alpha waves during most of a five-minute period. He said he had thought of an empty blue sky "with a small white cloud" occasionally passing by. He also said that "alpha isn't anything. It is literally nothing."

Next the swami was able to produce almost continuous theta waves during a five-minute period. Asked about this experience, he replied that it was "very noisy." He said that while this state of mind was useful, he usually kept it turned off because his subconscious mind would flood him with memories of people calling to him to do all sorts of things.

After the theta sessions the swami felt he understood the way in which his brain waves related to his internal states and offered to produce delta the next day. Dr. Green told him that in order to do so he would have to be asleep. The swami insisted that he would be able to produce delta but would still be aware of what was happening around him.

Next day Swami Rama began the test by lying down with his eyes closed and soon began to snore. He seemed to be asleep, and slow delta waves, those typical of deep sleep, soon appeared in the pen tracings. Mrs. Green was in the room with the swami. Without having told the swami beforehand, she began to speak quietly saying, "Today the sun is shining but tomorrow it may rain." Every five minutes she spoke another short sentence throughout the test, which lasted twenty-five minutes. The swami then woke up. He announced that someone on the floor above had made a clicking sound with sharp heels, and that elsewhere in the building he had heard doors slamming twice. He then amazed the researchers by repeating Mrs. Green's sentences almost word for word.

Although this unusual state had the characteristics of deep sleep, while in it the swami was able to retain awareness of all the sounds around him. He called it "yogic sleep" or "dog sleep." Like a dog, which is able to leap up wide awake from a sound sleep, the yogi could come out of it almost instantly alert without the groggy stages that usually come after deep sleep. The swami explained that for this experiment he had instructed his mind to be absolutely quiet. It was not to respond but simply to record everything until called upon later. This state was one that the swami found very beneficial since he felt only fifteen minutes of "yogic sleep" was worth as much as an hour of ordinary sleep.

In certain of his withdrawn states Swami Rama could pick up accurate information about the illnesses of people at a distance, the kind of clairvoyant diagnosis typical of a few gifted psychics. As is usually the case, the swami produced several of the brain-wave patterns at the same time. When he produced predominantly alpha waves, the beta waves would also continue. When theta waves predominated, both alpha and beta would appear, and with delta the other brain waves continued to be recorded as well. Dr. Green speculated that perhaps the particular combination of brain waves present during the swami's yogic sleep allowed him to remember what was happening around him.

Studies of brain-wave control at The Menninger Foundation suggested a relationship between brain waves and creativity. During regular training sessions some of the subjects slipped into a reverie in which dreamlike scenes and images appeared. The researchers, Elmer and Alyce

Green and Dale Walters, noticed that during such a reverie the subjects were often producing theta brain waves at about four to eight cycles per second. They knew that theta was typically present as a person approaches sleep and as a person approaches wakefulness.

Alyce Green had been doing a project on creativity. In a study of the lives of famous artists, writers, and scientists she discovered a commonly reported experience. Many creative people described a special state of mind in which rich images seemed to rush in, often bringing a new idea or a solution to a problem. Sometimes inspiration came in dreams. Other times it interrupted the usual flow of daytime thoughts with vivid images from the subconscious mind. Dr. and Mrs. Green realized that the experiences of their theta subjects were similar. The images seemed to appear by themselves and often seemed even more real than those of regular dreams.

Alpha waves seemed associated with an inner state of quiet awareness, and theta seemed associated with a deep inner state characterized by spontaneous images. Interested in these associations, Dr. and Mrs. Green undertook several new biofeedback projects. For one of these studies twenty-six male students were chosen from nearby Washburn University in Topeka. The complete experiment ran for ten weeks.

During the first five-week training period the students

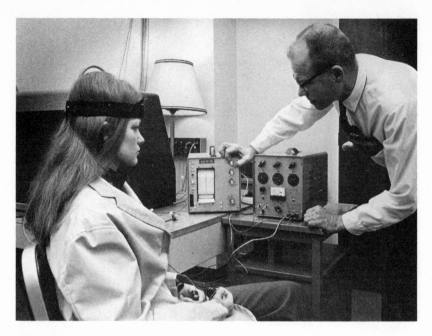

Dr. Elmer Green demonstrates
a portable brain-wave trainer to a subject
as her brain waves are recorded as a single tracing
on a paper strip in machine at left.
Wires attached to her hands
are for recording other physiological processes.

learned to increase the percentage of alpha and theta brain waves produced when their eyes were closed. Tone signals were used as feedback. A low tone signaled that theta waves were being produced; a higher tone meant that alpha was present. The task for each subject was to increase the amount of alpha and theta. Subjects were asked to notice and report their inner experiences.

The students came to the laboratory for training every other week. After being seated in a reclining chair in a quiet, dimly lit room, each subject practiced relaxation and rhythmic breathing. He then received simultaneous alpha and theta feedback for fifteen minutes. This period was followed by a period of theta feedback alone for thirty minutes. Three small rooms at Washburn University were set up as practice rooms with portable brain-wave machines, so that each subject could practice about an hour a day when away from the laboratory. The students kept diaries in which they recorded their experiences.

During the second five-week training period the same procedure was followed, but the students were asked to be especially concerned with increasing their theta brain waves, and to report the special imagery associated with this state. The researchers explained this "hypnogogic" imagery as that which suddenly comes to the mind from some unconscious source. It could be in the form of pictures, sounds, touch, taste, or smell, or any combination of sense impressions. In these last five weeks of training the subjects were briefly interrupted at various times by the researchers, using a special intercom system. When asked, "What is happening?" they could tell briefly what they were experiencing just before being interrupted.

As a result of the training, most of the students were

able to increase production of alpha waves easily. Production of theta was more difficult but also was increased. Of special interest was the increased ability of the students to experience and report the imagery associated with the theta state. Many reports indicated that the students felt more integrated as a result of the training. One subject said, "I have experienced generally, after sessions, a kind of speeding up. I feel good inside, physically things are in order and I just feel sharper, sharper. . . ." Another reported, "I'm calmer and I feel more at peace. . . ." Others described similar experiences such as, "I feel good after a session, like whatever I have to do, I can do," or, "I feel so put together."

Several students found exams easier to take after alpha-theta sessions. They felt more relaxed than usual and found that thoughts and memories seemed to fit together with less effort. Many reported an increased awareness of nature and a greater satisfaction in whatever they were doing. Symbols such as those found in dreams also seemed an important part of the students' experiences. Images of reaching the light at the end of a tunnel or of a "wise old man" seen as a teacher or doctor were reported. Another frequent image was that of a book containing special knowledge. One subject envisioned an office in which he was looking for some information. A large man he had never seen before came from behind some file cabinets with a paperback book saying, "The answer to everything you want to know is right in here." The subject described the book as containing Greek words, handwriting, and pictures. Recounting this experience, he said, "When I looked at the words I knew, 'That is the truth.' That's what I was after."

Some of the Menninger alpha-theta subjects reported ESP experiences. Several incidents were noted by one psychology student. His reveries began to include accurate images of the future. In one, an image appeared of a letter being delivered to his apartment with the news that he had been accepted into graduate school. His roommate gave him the good news at the door. When he actually went home later that day, there was his roommate at the door with the message he had visualized earlier.

Some people find the theta experience similar to a good "trip" with drugs. The difference is that the theta reverie is not externally induced, but is completely under the subject's own control. It is more natural and does not include the risk of introducing chemicals into the body. Some, like Swami Rama at the Menninger lab, feel the theta state is busy and upsetting. Most feel it is a positive experience. In it there are fresh inner events, rich memories, and sometimes unusual insights. And the combination of alpha and theta brain-wave production seems especially useful. Internal focus on such states through biofeedback may prove to be a way of tapping one's creative resources more quickly.

Biofeedback researchers also have become aware of the importance of brain waves being "in step" or "out of step." The jangling busyness of much activity is accompanied by brain waves that not only are high in frequency but usually irregular. At such times patterns from one area of the brain don't particularly match patterns from other areas. The brain is like a telephone switchboard where the operator is getting too many calls at the same time.

On the other hand, during biofeedback relaxation, some people synchronize their brain-wave patterns much the way a symphony orchestra produces harmonious music. Alpha waves may be generated in many parts of the brain at once. And the alpha pulses begin to synchronize or come "in phase," like the members of a marching band getting into step. Or sometimes alpha waves may be just twice as frequent as theta waves being produced at the same time, like the bottom and top notes of a musical scale, which blend into a harmonious sound. This blending of brain waves into unison or chords seems typical of a sense of calm and efficient control. Brain

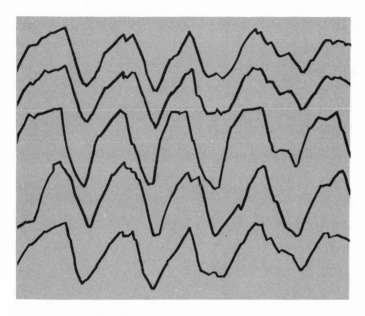

Peaks that coincide show
that brain waves from separate points on the head
are in synchrony, or in phase.

energies are reinforcing one another rather than working in conflict.

A scientist who stresses brain-wave synchrony is Dr. Lester Fehmi at Princeton Medical Center. Rather than training subjects to produce particular brain waves, Fehmi concentrates on training brain-wave synchrony. He teaches a subject to synchronize brain waves from different parts of the brain, using either alpha or theta frequency, depending on which is most natural. Each person, says Fehmi, has particular frequencies at which he or she produces the highest amplitude waves. Using this natural characteristic frequency, Fehmi helps his subjects to make their brain-wave patterns more regular and more synchronous, or "in step."

One of Fehmi's talented subjects is musician David Rosenboom. It was found that while Rosenboom was composing a symphony his brain waves showed large beta bursts that were multiples of lower frequencies.

EEG equipment for monitoring brain waves
is adjusted by Dr. Lester Fehmi.

These bursts coincided with moments of inspiration. Rosenboom became so successful at controlling his brain waves that he used them to give a biofeedback concert at Automation House in New York City. His brain waves were fed into an electronic music synthesizer. The result was a new kind of sound concert created directly by the brain's electrical activity. Musicians seem particularly sensitive to biofeedback signals heard as bleeps, tones,

Dr. Fehmi demonstrates an alpha training routine using a tone as biofeedback signal.

and pulsations. Accustomed to imagining sounds and rhythms, brain-wave control seems to them a partial extension of ordinary music making.

Fehmi has noticed that some of his subjects make fast progress with biofeedback while others are very slow. The more successful subjects reported certain feelings particularly associated with the relaxing alpha state. They often described an effortless flow of energy through mind and body, and they became aware of things outside or inside the body without straining. The usual frustrations and barriers seemed to disappear. Their state of mind was like Swami Rama's description of alpha as "nothing at all." Yet, at the same time, the field of awareness actually seemed to be expanded.

In helping his patients to speed alpha-state relaxation, Fehmi found certain images to be very effective. These images were put in the form of questions. "Can you imagine the distance between your eyes?" and "Can you imagine the distance between your ears?" To relax their concentration on objects, the patients were asked to focus on distances or something that was not there at all. Fehmi developed a complete set of such questions, which he calls "open focus."

Open focus moves gradually through the sections of the body, suggesting that all are full of space. The exercises continue with more general suggestions such as,

"Can you imagine that your whole being fills with air when you inhale and your whole being is left filled with space when you exhale, that the boundaries between the space inside and the space outside are dissolving, and that the space inside and the space outside become one continuous and unified space." There is a pause between each suggestion, and the whole procedure may take a half hour while the subject relaxes comfortably in a chair in a quiet room. The open-focus series can be read to a person or played back on a tape recorder perhaps once a day.

Those who spend regular time with open-focus relaxation prove more rapidly successful during the actual biofeedback training. Fehmi has also found that even lab visitors are stimulated by a simulated alpha-tone signal beeping in the background at about ten pulses per second, an imitation of an actual feedback signal.

Hypnosis, a state that shares some characteristics of open focus, seems to show promise for biofeedback training. The autogenic temperature system used at The Menninger Foundation grew out of relaxation suggestions that are often used in hypnosis. In a later experiment a connection was found between hypnosis and ability to learn brain-wave control. Dr. E. S. Paul Weber, at the Princeton Medical Center, placed a gifted hypnotic subject in trance. The subject, a woman, was wired for EEG recordings of her brain waves. A feedback tone signaled when she was producing alpha.

First Dr. Weber asked her to produce more tone, and then later to stop the tone. The hypnotized subject responded correctly. Then the equipment was adjusted to monitor theta brain waves with the feedback tone. Again the woman was able to control production of theta waves, turning the tone on or off. Finally she was asked to produce alpha from one location on her head and theta from another location at the same time. She not only did so correctly, she could also switch the alpha and theta signals between the two locations. In addition, she could produce any combination of the alpha and theta waves and turn them on and off when asked to do so.

This subject was unusually gifted, but the experiment suggests that under the proper conditions the learning of such control can be a rapid and natural process. Apparently the abilities tapped through biofeedback may already be present even without extended sessions requiring hours or weeks of training.

A New Science

The science of biofeedback has had to overcome many problems to establish itself. Most of the early experimenters at first worked alone. Some were psychologists, some were physiologists, others were medical doctors or psychiatrists. Because of sharply divided specialties, many investigators did not know that others were doing similar work and thinking along similar lines.

One of the first steps to establish communication among biofeedback researchers was taken by psychologist Lester Fehmi. In January of 1969 he invited Dr. Joe Kamiya, Dr. Thomas Mulholland, Dr. Thomas Budzinski, Dr. Barbara Brown, and other scientists to attend a conference dealing with voluntary control of inner body processes. Another effort at communication was made by Dr. Joseph Hart, who had been working with alpha-brain-wave training at the University of California at Irvine. He began circulating an information letter to scientists working in similar directions.

Later Dr. Joe Kamiya, Dr. Barbara Brown, Dr. Gardner Murphy, and Dr. Kenneth Gaarder sent out a questionnaire to explore interest in the idea. Response was amazing. There was so much curiosity that a national meeting was quickly scheduled. More than 140 professionals from various disciplines convened to share their interests in biofeedback. The Biofeedback Research Society was organized at that first meeting. Since then the new professional group has been constantly active, setting up biofeedback meetings and publishing the work of its members.

Not all scientists have been happy with the stir created by biofeedback. For years the behavioral psychologists, and most physical scientists as well, had accepted the idea that there was no such thing as independent human will. The common assumption was that personality was nothing more than patterns of habit and reaction built up by the past interaction of an organism with its environment. According to this view, people became conditioned to act in certain ways because of their constant reaction to what went on around them.

Results from biofeedback experiments partly upset this popular idea. Biofeedback demonstrated conscious control over inner body processes, affirming that the human will, or volition, was something real and important after all. Through biofeedback people were put in touch with parts of their selves that had seemed out of reach before, apparently enabling them to use a kind of passive volition to bring about certain useful changes.

So while some scientists were embracing the idea of biofeedback, others were busy writing it off as a fad that would pass. Meanwhile, the public learned about biofeedback through newspapers, magazines, and television. Even though biofeedback uses complicated electronic equipment, the basic idea is easy to understand. Researchers who had been looking for subjects suddenly found that enormous numbers of people were curious and willing to volunteer. Many were fascinated with the thought of changing their own body temperature or seeing and hearing their own brain waves.

Those looking for a profitable business jumped on the bandwagon. Advertisements appeared for "emotion meters," portable "alpha" devices, and training sessions to "put you in touch with your inner powers." Although less expensive than laboratory equipment, the machines were advertised as being able to do the same things.

In some cases, the equipment worked fairly well for the price. In other cases, it was so poorly designed that a so-called alpha machine might measure mostly background static or stray signals having nothing to do with actual alpha brain waves. And some courses claimed to teach relaxation through "alpha" without the use of monitoring equipment.

Many companies producing high-quality laboratory equipment now offer moderately priced units as well. Yet there is little standardization, and one must be very well informed in order to select home-use equipment that will really work. A good plan is to ask advice from a professional who is familiar with biofeedback research and the wide variety of equipment before buying any electronic feedback devices. Also, numerous hospitals and universities around the country and in other parts of the world have developed training facilities open both to patients and the general public. Sometimes portable equipment can be borrowed or rented for home use.

One of the greatest worries of the researchers, however, is that claims about biofeedback have been exaggerated. Too much has been expected by the public. Under the right conditions, biofeedback does a certain job in a new way. But it cannot do everything and is probably most effective when combined with other forms of training and treatment. One of the problems for the researchers has been to pinpoint those results that can be credited to biofeedback and not other factors.

Sometimes successful biofeedback experiments have proved hard to duplicate. Researchers Neal Miller and Leo DiCara found such a problem in training laboratory rats. In early experiments the rats had done well in the task of learning to control heart rate and other internal functions. But in later experiments the results were not encouraging. Some of the problems may have been due to changes in the breeding and handling of new laboratory rats. Even the special curare chemical could vary somewhat from batch to batch. Further studies were necessary.

In other biofeedback experiments results seemed good, but often the methods were not precise enough. To be complete, each experiment should have a control group as well as the group receiving biofeedback training. If the control group, which receives no feedback training, still shows some learning or improvement, then factors other than biofeedback are also at work.

To try to solve some of these problems, David Walsh set up a special alpha brain-wave program. Four different procedures were devised for four different groups of psychology students. Each group was placed in a light- and soundproof room. The first group received alpha instructions—explanation of what alpha is and how they might feel—along with real alpha feedback. Group two received alpha instructions with no feedback. Group three had some general instructions about brain waves with real alpha feedback. And group four received neutral instructions and no alpha feedback.

Only those subjects who received both alpha instructions and real alpha feedback actually experienced an alpha state. In Walsh's experiment, the subjects needed more than alpha feedback. They also needed to understand the nature of alpha brain waves and just what they might expect to happen.

A criticism of biofeedback experiments has been that some of the results might be due to a placebo effect. The word *placebo* comes from the Latin for *please*. It is used when a doctor prescribes a drug that has no active ingredient; it may be sugar or some other harmless chemical having no effect one way or another. The word *placebo* may also be used to describe a procedure followed not because of its real value but because the patient believes in it. Belief is such a strong factor that many patients do improve with such techniques.

Do patients sometimes improve only because of their belief that biofeedback will help them and not because of the method itself? Psychologist Lester Fehmi designed an experiment to assess the effectiveness of biofeedback training independent of placebo effect. He used what is called a "double-blind" procedure in which neither the experimenters nor the subjects know beforehand which parts of the tests are real and which are simulated.

First twenty business managers were chosen from a group answering a newspaper ad. All received twenty sessions of alpha-feedback training. They were told only that the experiment used biofeedback and had to do with mental attention. Using random groupings chosen before-hand, the subjects were paired up for each session. In each pair one subject would receive his own actual alpha feedback. The other subject would receive either the feed-back of his partner or a previously taped recording of his partner's alpha. During the tests neither the experi-menter nor his assistants knew which subjects were get-ting their own real feedback and which subjects were getting the bogus feedback.

During test periods the subjects were repeatedly in-structed to "turn the tone on," to "rest," and to "turn the tone off." By the end of the experiment those who had been getting real feedback had learned to turn their alpha on or off. The control subjects getting bogus feedback had not learned to do so. In addition, the subjects getting their own feedback showed a higher level of alpha during the rest periods. These successful subjects rated them-selves as being calmer, more able to concentrate, and more satisfied with life than they had been before the training. The control subjects did not feel the same im-provements and actually rated themselves as being more distracted and less satisfied with life than before. Some of the subjects receiving real feedback also reported feel-ing better physically as well.

This particular double-blind experiment produced pos-itive evidence for the effectiveness of biofeedback training apart from its placebo effect. Many more of these highly controlled tests are needed in order for biofeedback to become generally accepted by the scientific community as a proven method.

Dr. Fehmi stresses attention as the key process in EEG biofeedback training. His successful subjects have gained a flexible control over their attention, concentration, and focus. They score better on psychological tests that measure these abilities. At the same time they have learned to let awareness shift from one mental state to another without blocking these shifts. They find themselves more aware of what is happening around themselves. They feel that they get along with other people better.

In the earliest biofeedback experiments scientists examined body functions separately to find out how they were affected by biofeedback training. The more a process could be isolated, the better the chance of finding out just what was happening. But even in these single experiments, the real joy for the volunteers was that in some way mind and body came together whereas they had seemed split apart before. There was the feeling of experiencing the action in the muscles or the heart or the bloodstream, a recognition of oneself as a complete whole.

And it was not just unfamiliar body parts that were being discovered, but unfamiliar parts of the mind as well. These layers of mental activity had been there all the time, but had never seemed well acquainted with each other. And almost miraculously, as these boundaries within the self broke down, the boundaries outside the self seemed also to disappear.

Biofeedback has made available new information about subconscious perception. It has been known that at the subconscious level a person may register an impression that is too brief to be noticed by the conscious mind. And without understanding it, the person may make a decision and take action on this subconscious information.

For example, in the middle of a movie, still pictures of a glass of water can be flashed at intervals so quickly that nobody in the theater even notices their presence. However, the brief images are registered by the subconscious mind. And without really knowing why, a number of people will feel thirsty and go to the lobby to look for a water fountain or drink machine. This ability of the subconscious to detect information below the usual threshold of awareness is called subliminal perception.

Dr. David Kahn devised an ingenious biofeedback project in subliminal perception. Skin electrodes were used to pick up muscle-cell firing. The pulses operated strobe lights that flashed pictures on a screen. Ordinarily the flashes were too short for the pictures to be recognized at the conscious level. Some of the pictures were pleasant while others were horrifying. The subjects learned to increase muscle firing gradually in order to bring the pleasant pictures into conscious view, while they turned off the muscle firing to avoid looking at the unpleasant scenes.

In this case, the subconscious was running the show. It was perceiving what the conscious could not, reacting to the scenes, and working as a guardian to decide in advance what the conscious mind should or should not be allowed to see. Thus, the biofeedback training was working even without the knowledge of the conscious mind.

The same thing may possibly happen in dreams during deep sleep. There the subconscious selects images to be communicated to the outer conscious level. Biofeedback suggests that all these levels are constantly at work and while one or another may dominate at times, the overall result is what matters.

Researchers have noticed that certain kinds of people make better biofeedback subjects than others. For instance, in brain-wave training artists and athletes tend to be good alpha producers. Joe Kamiya has also noticed that people who focus attention inwards learn to increase alpha quickly. They are people who, Kamiya says, use words like *images, dreams, wants,* and *feelings.*

In addition, many researchers report high success with subjects who have practiced some kind of meditation. One popular form is Zen Buddhism, which comes from Japan. Akira Kasamatsu and Tomie Hirai tested subjects who had various amounts of Zen training. Those with a number of years of experience produced similar brain-wave patterns during meditation.

Ordinarily alpha waves are present only occasionally during the waking state and increase when the eyes are closed. In the case of the Zen meditators, strong alpha came shortly after the start of meditation even though the eyes were kept open. Gradually the alpha became stronger. After about twenty-five minutes of meditation, the alpha waves began to slow from around eleven per second to around seven or eight per second. And soon rhythmic theta pulses at around six or seven per second began to appear. Even after completion of meditation, alpha waves continued for several minutes as an after-effect. Somehow such trained meditators reach body relaxation even greater than that during sleep and yet remain fully alert. Whether the approach is Zen, Yoga, TM, Open Focus, or some other self-relaxation or meditative technique, such practices seem to enable the subject to make the most of biofeedback training.

Although it may be most helpful to particular kinds of people, biofeedback can make important contributions to education in general. The ability to apply oneself and to shift attention easily, and the capacity for increased awareness are at the foundation of all learning and self-improvement, and these skills are trainable through bio-feedback. Dr. Lester Fehmi suggests that once accepted as a useful method, biofeedback may take its place as another important educational tool.

New materials may be useful for biofeedback. For example, certain synthetic liquid crystals change color as temperature changes. One kind of liquid crystal has been marketed as a "mood ring," which changes color with variations in hand temperature. While little more than a curiosity now, the refinement of such temperature-sensitive techniques may make possible simpler low-cost bio-feedback devices for personal use.

New electrical measurements at the surface of the body offer promise for biofeedback. A device called a tobi-scope now can locate the points on the body traditionally associated with acupuncture. There is low skin resistance at these points, which can be stimulated with fine needles and a small electric charge for therapeutic purposes such as dulling pain. The points are small and precise and may expand in diameter with emotional excitability. When a point is located, the tobiscope light turns on.

Magnetic and electrical fields around the body now can be monitored with special equipment. Radiation-field photography makes possible colored pictures of electron flow through fields radiating from fingertips and other body surfaces. Much like the skin-sensitive measurements of the GSR, radiation-field photographs seem to reflect ongoing changes of mood and body systems. Apparently changes in the body field can even give advance warning of illness that takes physical form later. As scientists find ways of translating such measurements into continuous pictures, these signals too may be useful for biofeedback.

Though still in its beginnings as a science, the potential for bringing body and mind together through biofeedback seems unlimited. Almost every way of measuring the interior activity of body, brain, or mind seems to offer new possibilities for self-improvement and for scientific discovery.

Index

*indicates illustration

The idea that people can control involuntary body functions through an effort of will has long been held in Oriental cultures. Now it has achieved new currency in the West under the name of biofeedback. Here Larry Kettelkamp explores the ramifications of the young science, reporting on the insights and procedures it has contributed to medicine, psychotherapy, learning theory, and creativity research.

Separate chapters describe experiments with heart rate, blood pressure, body temperature, muscle contraction, and brainwave frequency. Apparently all these processes can be consciously regulated when subjects are able to monitor their progress with external signals. Thus a woman can learn to banish a migraine headache by sending blood from her head—reducing pressure there—to warm her cold hands; a man can learn to stabilize an irregular heartbeat by watching a light that registers his success.

Explaining the mechanics of biofeedback and considering its wide-reaching implications, Larry Kettelkamp has provided another book that is informative, stimulating, and provocative, a must for anyone interested in relationships between mind and body.